Write Your Novel
From The Middle

JAMES SCOTT BELL

Compendium Press

Table of Contents

1. Pantser, Meet Plotter and Say Hello To Tweener

Pam Pantser loves writing so much she'd do it even if she never got published or paid. Even if she never landed a contract or sold anything online. For her it's about the writing itself—getting up each day and going wherever her imagination leads.

Of course, she'd actually like a little income from her writing. Who wouldn't? She once tried to outline a novel. It almost killed her. Her wild writer's mind kept fighting her, telling her she was actually hurting all that was good and lovely and true in her writing. She pressed on with the outline, but it was like shampooing a porcupine.

Then she read an article where some author said all outlining is bovine droppings (he used a different word) and anybody who tells you to use an outline is a fraud. This warmed Pam's heart so much she ditched her outline and entered NaNoWriMo with only a wing and a prayer. One month later she had what she called a "novel." But when she looked at it in January she couldn't make out what kind of novel it was. She showed it to one of her best friends in the world, Cathy Critique. Cathy actually took Pam to lunch and insisted on paying. Because she had to tell Pam that, while there were some beautiful paragraphs and lines, the story was dull, unfocused, meandering and, to put it bluntly, "a mess."

"I know that!" Pam said. "But I'm a pantser! What am I supposed to do? I can't outline to save my life! Am I doomed?"

Cathy, even though insisting Pam have an entire chocolate soufflé for herself, had no answer for Pam.

But I do.

Paul Plotter could build you a bridge across a gorge. His mind is a steel trap, a Rubik's Cube, a filled-out crossword puzzle. He can map out a story like Lewis and Clark charting the Louisiana Purchase. His outlines have a perfect three acts, The Hero's Journey in all its glory, and hit every mark on the Blake Snyder Beat Sheet. He has self-published nine thrillers, all of them getting reviews like, "Pretty darn good" and "Nicely paced."

But none of his novels have taken off. He can't figure out why.

He has tried to emulate James Patterson. He heard once that Patterson works (or at least used to work) from outlines that are sometimes eighty pages long.

Paul's outlines are works of art, and if there was a market for outlines he's pretty sure he could make a living as a writer.

And you should see his character backgrounds! The man writes page after page of backstory for his main characters, and even fills out questionnaires on his minor ones. In fact, Paul likes to carry around a fat binder full of all his pages of outlining, character work, and research. He likes it when people at

Starbucks ask him what's in the binder. He can talk for hours on the benefits of outlining.

But somewhere between complete outline and finished novel, something doesn't jell. For some reason, Paul's perfectly plotted stories don't catch fire.

He's read a million words of craft advice, taken classes live and online. He knows his stuff, but doesn't know how to take it to the next level.

I'm going to help Paul.

Tammy Tweener falls somewhere in the middle of Pam and Paul. She knows them both, and sometimes has coffee with them. Separately, of course. Pam rubs Paul the wrong way, and Paul thinks Pam is a little to "precious." But Tammy is a free spirit who can get along with both, because she mostly listens, smiles, and nods.

She sometimes laughs at Pam's idealism and Paul's cocksureness.

She herself has taken a page from each. She outlines a little. She has key story beats she knows she must hit. But she also likes to keep things loose in between, to "let the story breathe."

If you talk to her alone, she might tell you she has days she feels the exhilaration of Pam, and other days when she feels in total control, like Paul.

But she has a problem with her finished novels, too. She has this dull, aching, indefinable feeling that there's a deeper story in there somewhere. But for the life of her she can't figure out where to look to find it.

I will show her where to look.

I have been studying, practicing and teaching the craft of writing for over twenty years. I've written several books for Writer's Digest Books, dozens of articles for *Writer's Digest* magazine, blogged, and held seminars and workshops all over. In all that time I believe this may be the single most powerful writing strategy I have ever developed. Because it works at *any stage of your writing,* whether you are a plotter, a pantser or a tweener.

Sometimes you'll hear writers say they like to start at the beginning and just see where things lead.

Others say they like to know the end, and then have the "fun" of writing to get there.

Either approach is fine, but what I'm suggesting in this book is even better, more powerful, and will be immensely pleasing to you as an author.

I am going to suggest is that you write from the middle and work outward from there.

What? The middle?

That's right. The dead center. Because that's where you're going to discover *what your story is really all about.*

It's also going to deepen your novel and clarify it in a way that will amaze you and—more importantly--your readers.

So, you like pantsing? Have at it! And know that at any time you can head to the middle and find a clarity of purpose that will send your spontaneous soul soaring.

Outliner? The middle is where your true "superstructure" is going to be found. Don't ever try to complete an outline without it again.

Big claims, but I'm prepared to back them up in this book.

But first, let me tell you how I came up with this Write From the Middle Method.

2. Beginning, End or Middle?

A few years ago, after nearly two decades of craft study and teaching, I decided to give some concentrated thought to what writing teachers call the "midpoint." I'd read about it in craft books and blogs, but never found the discussions particularly useful. Everyone identified midpoint as a scene of some kind, after which something changes. But what? And why?

To me, Act II is all about rising action, the battle with death stakes (see the next chapter) and I figured you should write about this rising action all the way to Act III.

Structurally, that's true. But I still wanted to know if there was something everyone, including me, might be missing with the midpoint idea.

So I decided to take a few favorite movies and slide the timer on the DVD player to the exact middle.

Then I chose some favorite novels and opened up to the middles of their page counts.

I snooped around in those spots, never veering very far to the right or the left.

And what I found there literally knocked my socks off. Yes, I actually had to go around my house picking up my own socks, so amazing was this discovery.

What I found was that this midpoint was not a scene at all.

It is a *moment* within a scene.

Not only that. The midpoint moment (which I fully explain in Chapter 5) is the moment that *tells us what the novel or movie is really all about.*

You see, the character is going to have to face a death of some kind in the story. There are three kinds of death and one or more will confront the character, in bold relief, right smack dab in the middle of your novel.

Let me explain this death thing a little further in the next chapter. Then I need to give you some basics of structure (Chapter 4) in order to set up the discussion of the midpoint (Chapter 5).

3. Make Sure the Stakes Are Life and Death

A great novel is the record of how a character fights with *death*.

That's right, death. Somebody has to be in danger of dying, and that someone is the Lead character.

Now, before you category romance authors start throwing bookmarks at me, note: There are three kinds of death: physical, professional, psychological. One or more of these must be present in your novel if it's going to work at the optimum level.

Let's take a look at each.

Physical

Obviously if your Lead character in danger of physical death, the stakes are as high as they can be. Usually you find this in the thriller genre. Bad guy wants to kill good guy.

Somebody always wants to kill Jack Reacher.

In Alfred Hitchcock's *North By Northwest*, bad spies mistakenly identify Roger Thornhill (Cary Grant) as an enemy spy. They spend the rest of the movie trying to kill him.

Professional

When the novel revolves around the Lead's calling in life, the failure to win should mean that her career is over, her calling a waste, her training a fraud, her future a cloud. It must mean that there is something on the line here that will make or break the Lead in the area of her life's work.

This is the thread that makes Michael Connelly's Harry Bosch series so compelling. Harry has a working rule that obsesses him. As he puts it in *The Last Coyote*, "Everybody counts or nobody counts. That's it. It means I bust my ass to make a case whether it's a prostitute or the mayor's wife. That's my rule."

For Harry, there's no getting around this drive, so every case becomes a matter of solving it or *dying professionally*. He is in danger of being drummed off the force at times, or in not being able to go on.

Make the job and the particular case matter that much. A lawyer with the one client he needs to vindicate (as in Barry Reed's *The Verdict*, made into the hit movie starring Paul Newman); the trainee whose law enforcement career could be over before it begins (as in Thomas Harris's *The Silence of the Lambs*); a cop with a last chance case involving horrific killings (*The Night Gardener* by George Pelecanos.

Psychological

Dying on the inside. We say that about certain events. We should say it about the Lead character. Imminent danger of dying psychologically if the conflict isn't won.

Holden Caulfield in *The Catcher in the Rye*. If he doesn't find authenticity in the world, he's going to die psychologically (does he? At the end, we're not sure, but it's close). In fact, if he doesn't find this reason, we're pretty sure actual death—by suicide—is inevitable.

Psychological death is crucial to understand, as it elevates the emotions of fiction like no other aspect.

Another example comes from the classic Bette Davis movie, *Now, Voyager*. In this film Bette plays a woman who has been kept under the thumb of the ruthless matriarch of an upper crust Boston family. She's been told she's ugly, without charm or talent, and is turned into a complete recluse.

But when her psychiatrist sends her on a cruise, alone, she meets a man who begins to draw her out. She comes back to Boston with new confidence, and immediately her mother tries to take it away.

Will she be able to break away and become a fully realized woman? If she doesn't, she dies on the inside. Her life will be, functionally, over.

Psychological death is the key to all romances, isn't it? If the two lovers don't get together, they will each miss out on their "soul mate." Their lives will be incurably damaged. Since readers of traditional romances know they're going to end up together, it's all the more important to create this illusion of imminent psychological death.

This is also the secret to lighter fare. The people in the comedy need to think they're in a tragedy, usually over something trivial. But the "something trivial" has to matter so much to the characters that *they* believe they will suffer psychological "death" if they don't gain their objective.

For example, Oscar Madison in *The Odd Couple* loves being a happy-go-lucky slob. He loves not cleaning up his apartment, smoking and eating whenever he wants, having poker games at all hours and so on. When neat freak Felix Unger moves in, that life Oscar loves so much is threatened. In Oscar's mind it's so bad he gets close to wanting to kill Felix.

Being a happy slob matters to Oscar. We believe it even though it's trivial, and there's the comedy.

You can have more than one aspect of death going on in your novel, but one is usually primary. In *The Fugitive,* physical death is at stake for most of the movie. If Dr. Richard Kimble is captured he goes to Death Row. He may be shot by law enforcement.

But there is a second thread, the psychological. Richard Kimble wants justice for his wife. But staying alive is his main problem.

Know your death stakes! This is going to be crucial in order for you to write your novel from the middle.

Now I want to take one more excursion into structure, and explain the two main pillars, because that sets us up for understanding the midpoint in all its glory.

4. The Two Pillars

Structure is translation software for your imagination.

You, the writer, have a story you want to tell. You feel it, see it, populate it with characters.

You start to put it on paper, or onscreen. This is your material, and you have to "translate" it into a form that readers can relate to.

That's what structure does. To the extent you ignore it or mess with it, you risk frustrating—or worse, turning off—readers.

That's not something you want to do too much of if you desire to have a writing career.

I was amused many years ago when a writing teacher of some repute shouted in front of an auditorium that there was no such thing as structure. He went on and on about this.

Later, looking at his materials and the terms he had made up for various story beats, guess how they unfolded? Yep, in a perfect, three-act structure.

Thus, writers who like to outline can set up a strong story just by mapping out a few key structural scenes.

But what if you're a writer who likes flying by the seat of the pants? No problem. Be as free as you like when creating material. Write hot.

Just understand that eventually you'll have to think about structuring all that writing, because manuscripts that ignore structure are almost always filed under *Unsold*.

And while it is true some authors purposely play with structure (some to the point their books are called "experimental") they usually know exactly why they are doing so. And they accept as a consequence that their books might not be as popular with the reading public as novels that have structure working for them.

At the very least understand structure fully before playing around with it. (This advice also applies to hand grenades).

My favorite visual image for structure is the suspension bridge.

As you can see, it looks like the three-act structure.

Why three? Think about it. Every story has to begin, and every story has to end. And in the middle it has to hold the reader's interest.

The craft of structure tells you how to begin with a bang, knock them out at the end, and keep them turning pages all the way through.

The key foundational elements here are the two pillars, or pylons. These pillars are set down in bedrock, allowing the suspension cables to support a solid and secure platform—the bridge itself.

When you ignore structure, your novel can begin to feel like one of those rope bridges swinging wildly in the wind over a 1000-foot gorge. Not many readers are going to want to go across.

The First Pillar

The beginning of a novel tells us who the main characters are and the situation at hand (the story world). It sets the tone and the stakes. But the novel does not take off or become "the story" until that first pillar is passed.

I call this a Doorway of No Return. The feeling must be that your Lead character, once she passes through, cannot go home again until the major problem of the plot is solved.

Let's take *Gone With the Wind* as our example.

In the first act, Scarlett O'Hara is sitting on her porch flirting with Brent and Stuart Tarleton. We get to know her as a selfish, scheming, privileged antebellum coquette. She is able to use her charms to enrapture the men around her and play them like carp on a hook. The mother of the Tarleton twins says Scarlett is "a fast piece if ever I saw one."

Now, if this novel were a thousand pages of Scarlett's flirtatious ways, we'd never make it past page ten. A successful novel is about *high stakes trouble*. True character is only revealed in crisis, so Margaret Mitchell gives us some opening trouble (what I call the Opening Disturbance)—Scarlett learns that Ashley is going to marry Melanie!

That trouble might be enough for a category romance, but not for a sprawling epic of the Old South. There must be something that forces Scarlett into a fight for her very way of life, and that's what the first pillar is about: it thrusts Scarlett into Act II.

That event is, of course, the outbreak of the Civil War.

On page 127 of my copy of *Gone With the Wind*, Charles Hamilton hastens to Scarlett at the big barbeque at Twelve Oaks:

"Have you heard? Paul Wilson just rode over from Jonesboro with the news!"

He paused, breathless, as he came up to her. She said nothing and only stared at him.

"Mr. Lincoln has called for men, soldiers—I mean volunteers—seventy-five thousand of them!"

The South, of course, sees this as provocation. Charles tells Scarlett it will mean fighting. "But don't you fret, Miss Scarlett, it'll be over in a month and we'll have them howling."

The Civil War is a shattering occurrence Scarlett cannot ignore or wish away. She would rather stay in the Old South and preserve Tara, her family home, and the way of life she grew up in.

In mythic terms, Scarlett would like to remain in the "ordinary world." But the outbreak of war *forces* Scarlett into the "dark world" of Act II.

That's why I call this a doorway of *no return.* There is no way back to the old, comfortable world. Scarlett has to face major troubles now. Not just about matters of the heart. She will need to save her family and her land. She will need money and cleverness. She must overcome or be overcome.

Act II is all about "death stakes." That is, one of three aspects of death must be on the line. Physical, professional or psychological death.

For Scarlett, it's psychological death (though her life is in danger at various points). If she doesn't preserve Tara and her vision of the Old South, she will "die inside." *Gone With the Wind*'s story question is: will Scarlett grow from her old self to the self she needs to be?

She doesn't want this fight. But she is pushed into the death stakes because of the war.

Other examples of the first pillar:

In *The Silence of the Lambs* Clarice Starling is thrust into a cat-and-mouse game with Hannibal Lecter because it might be the only way to solve a serial killer case.

In a PI (private investigator) novel, it's often when the detective takes on a client, as Sam Spade does with Brigid O'Shaughnessy in *The Maltese Falcon.*

In *To Kill a Mockingbird,* Atticus Finch accepts the job of defending a black man accused of raping a white girl. For Scout Finch, the narrator, this event thrusts her into a dark world of prejudice and injustice. She can't remain an innocent.

The timing of the first pillar should be before the 1/5 mark of your book. In movies, it's common to divide the acts into a 1/4 (Act I) 1/2 (Act II) and 1/4 (Act III) structure. But in novels it's better to have that first doorway happen earlier. In a fast moving action novel like *The Hunger Games*, it can happen quickly. It's in Chapter 2 that Katniss hears her sister's name chosen for the games, and immediately volunteers to take her place.

Gone With the Wind is over 1000 pages. The Civil War breaks out at about the 1/10 mark.

Look at your own novel:

- Have you given us a character worth following?

- Have you created a disturbance in the opening pages?

- Do you know the death stakes of the story?

- Have you created a scene that will force the character into the confrontation of Act II?

- Is it strong enough? Can the Lead character resist going into the battle?

- Does it occur before the 1/5 mark of your total page count?

The Second Pillar

The second pillar is Doorway of No Return #2. It is so designated because, once again, there is no going back (who would want to go back to continual trouble?) The Lead passes through this door *which makes possible or inevitable* the final battle and resolution.

Act II is where the major action takes place. The stakes are death (physical, professional or psychological) and the Lead has to fight. Remember, the first door has been slammed shut.

The second act is a series of actions where the character confronts and resists death and is opposed by counter forces.

In *Gone With the Wind*, Scarlett has many battles.

She needs to get out of Atlanta with Melanie before the Yankees take over.

She needs to get money to save Tara from onerous taxes.

She needs to figure out how to handle that charmer, Rhett Butler, who keeps showing up in her life.

And so on. All of these matters relate to the overall story question, the growth of Scarlett O'Hara.

Then the second pillar, or doorway, happens. It is an event that feels like a major crisis or setback. Or it can be a clue or discovery. The second pillar pushes the Lead character into Act III. It forces the final battle, the resolution. Indeed, makes that resolution possible.

In *Gone With the Wind*, the second pillar is a crisis. It occurs when Scarlett marries Rhett. This is a setback because Scarlett believes *she belonged to Ashley, forever and ever.* So why does she say yes to Rhett? Because it *was almost as if he had willed the word and she had spoken it without her own volition.* This marriage is going to make inevitable the final battle in Scarlett's heart. The crisis intensifies. Rhett finally realizes Scarlett will never give up on Ashley, and decides to leave the marriage. Scarlett, however, has a final realization of her own: she has been living for false dreams, and that home and Rhett are what she truly needs. But it will, of course, be too late. Rhett doesn't give a damn, and Scarlett will have to go back to Tara to think about getting him back. Tomorrow.

Examples of the second pillar:

Lecter tells Clarice that Buffalo Bill covets what he sees every day. (Clue) This information leads her to the killer.

The bullet-riddled body of a bundle-carrying ship's captain collapses in Sam Spade's office. Inside the bundle is the black bird. (Major discovery)

Tom Robinson, an innocent black man, is found guilty of rape by an all white jury, despite the evidence (set-back).

Look at your own novel:

Have you created a major crisis or setback the Lead must overcome?

Alternatively, is there a clue or discovery that makes a final resolution possible?

The Three Act structure, supported by the two strong pillars, will never let you down. It will guarantee that the platform of your story is strong. And it will free you to be as creative as you like with characters, voice and scenes without fear of falling off a rope bridge into the Valley of Unread Novels.

And now I'm going to tell you about the most amazing tool of all. It's the key to the Write From the Middle Method. And it works magic in your story. That's the subject of the next chapter.

5. The Magical Midpoint Moment

As I mentioned earlier, I started watching movies and looking at novels with this thing called the "midpoint" in mind. What I found was a *moment* in the middle of these stories that pulled together the entire narrative. The name I gave it is the "look in the mirror" moment. This is what it looks like within the three-act structure:

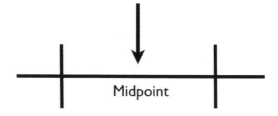

At this point in the story, the character looks at himself. He takes stock of where he is in the conflict and—depending on the type of story—has either of two basic thoughts. In a character-driven story, he looks at himself and wonders what kind of person he is. What is he becoming? If he continues the fight of

Act II, how will he be different? What will he have to do to overcome his inner challenges? How will he have to change in order to battle successfully?

The second type of look is more for plot-driven fiction. It's where the character looks at himself and considers the odds against him. At this point the forces seem so vast that there is virtually no way to go on and not face certain death. That death can be physical, professional, or psychological.

These two basic thoughts are not mutually exclusive. For example, an action story may be given added heft by incorporating the first kind of reflection into the narrative. This happens in *Lethal Weapon* when Riggs bares his soul to Murtaugh, admitting that killing people is "the only thing I was ever good at."

A few more examples may help.

In *Casablanca*, at the exact midpoint of the film, Ilsa comes to Rick's saloon after closing time. Rick has been getting drunk, remembering with bitterness what happened with him and Ilsa in Paris. Ilsa tries to explain why she left him in Paris, that she found out her husband Viktor Lazlo was still alive. She pleads with him to understand. But Rick is so bitter he basically calls her a whore. She weeps and leaves. And Rick, full of self-disgust, puts his head in his hands. He is thinking, "What have I become?" The rest of the film will determine whether he stays a selfish drunk, or regains his humanity. That, in fact, is what *Casablanca* is truly about, in both narrative and theme.

In *The Fugitive*, an action film, at the very center point of the movie Dr. Kimble is awakened in the basement room he's renting, by cops swarming all over the place.

He thinks they are after him, but it turns out they are actually after the son of the landlord. But the damage is done. Kimble breaks down. He is looking at the odds, thinking there's no way he can win this fight. There are too many resources arrayed against him.

To test this theory further, I looked for the midpoint of *Gone With The Wind,* the novel. I opened to the middle of the book and started searching. And there it was. At the end of Chapter 15, Scarlett looks inside herself, realizing that no one else but she can save Tara.

The trampled acres of Tara were all that was left to her, now that Mother and Ashley were gone, now that Gerald was senile from shock . . . security and position had vanished overnight. As from another world she remembered a conversation with her father about the land and wondered how she could have been so young, so ignorant, as not to understand what he meant when he said that the land was the one thing in the world worth fighting for...

Scarlett wonders what kind of person she has to become in order to save Tara. And the decision is made in the last paragraph:

Yes, Tara was worth fighting for, and she accepted simply and without question the fight. No one was going to get Tara away from her. No one was going to send her and her people adrift on the charity of relatives. She would hold Tara, if she had to break the back of every person on it.

And that is the essence of *Gone With The Wind.* It's the story of a young Southern belle who is forced (via a Doorway of No Return called The Civil War) to save her family home.

Also, notice how this is different from other definitions of the midpoint you'll see. Virtually all books on the craft approach it as another "plot" point. Something *external* happens that changes the course of the story. But what I detect is a *character point,* something *internal,* which has the added benefit of bonding audience and character on a deeper level.

When studying this, I grabbed three of my favorite movies at random and went to their midpoints. Here's what I found:

In *Moonstruck,* right smack dab in the middle, is the scene where Loretta goes into the confessional, because she has "slept with the brother of my fiancé." The priest says, "That's a pretty big sin." Loretta says, "I know . . ." And the priest tells her, "Reflect on your life!" He is actually instructing her to look in the mirror!

There's a perfect Mirror Moment in *It's a Wonderful Life.* It's the moment where Mr. Potter offers George Bailey a well-paid position with his firm, a job that will mean security for George's growing family. In return, though, George will have to give up the Building & Loan his father started. Potter offers George a cigar and George asks for time to think it over. He is actually requesting look-in-the-mirror time, and is seriously considering this move. Then he shakes Potter's hand, and the oily exchange suddenly clarifies what's at stake for him as a person. "No," he says, "now wait a minute here. I don't need twenty-four hours. I don't have to talk to anybody. I know right now, and the answer's no!" George had to make a decision as to what kind of man he was going to be. And he chose not to become another Potter.

Finally, in *Sunset Boulevard,* in the middle of the movie *to the minute,* Joe Gillis also has to decide what kind of man he is. Norma Desmond, his benefactor and lover, has tried to kill herself because Joe found a girl his own age that he wants to start seeing. When Joe hears about it he rushes back to her mansion with the thought that he'll finally tell her it's over, that he's leaving. But she threatens to attempt suicide again. And Joe sits down, literally, next to a mirror. In that moment he makes his fateful decision, the one that drives the rest of the movie.

More book examples:

In the middle of *The Silence of the Lambs,* Clarice is alone in her room, having just heard of Chilton's betrayal of Lecter, meaning she won't get any more information from him, meaning the certain death of the kidnapped girl she's been trying to save. The odds are now firmly against her and the FBI. In the shower, Clarice reflects back on a childhood memory which symbolizes loss for her.

At the midpoint of *The Hunger Games,* Katniss accepts the fact that she's going to die. The odds are too great:

I know the end is coming. My legs are shaking and my heart is too quick . . . . My fingers stroke the smooth ground, sliding easily across the top. This is an okay place to die, I think.

And, if I may, in the exact middle of my thriller, *Try Dying,* the narrator, Ty Buchanan, has just had his home firebombed. His fiancé has been murdered. And he reflects on two kinds of people, those who keep driving toward something, and those who have "given up the fight."

The question I had, and couldn't answer, was which kind was I?

Since I incorporated "look in the mirror moment" into my workshops, students have reported that it has been incredibly helpful. What it does is home in on what the story is really all about. The nice thing is you can explore this moment at any time in your writing process. You can play with it, tweak it. Whether you are a plotter or pantser, just thinking about what the "look in the mirror" might reveal will help you bring depth and cohesion to your novel.

That's why it's a magic moment.

And that's a key word, *moment.* The true midpoint is not a scene. It's a moment within a scene. It's like the earth's core. The true center. Find it in your novel, and everything will radiate from it.

By the way, I'm not sure that Margaret Mitchell, Suzanne Collins, or the writers of *Casablanca* were necessarily intentional about their midpoint moments. What I *am* saying is that their instincts as great storytellers put it there just the same. Could the reason these books and movies are classics, and others not, be the power of the look in the mirror?

My purpose in this book is to pop the hood and take a look at the engine, and offer you a way to build your own midpoint *intentionally*, so you truly can write your novel from the middle.

At any stage of your writing you can ask yourself what the Mirror Moment in your story might be. You can play with it. You can brainstorm. Is it a transformational moment? Is it about facing the toughest odds? What's going on *inside your character?* What do *you* want there to be going on?

This is the apex of what I call The Golden Triangle. This is the most crucial thing to know, because this is what your story is *really all about.*

Mirror Moment

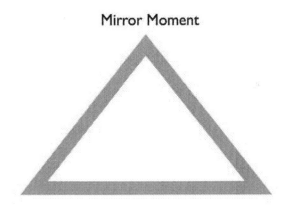

Once you know what the moment is, you can truly write from the middle. Because now you know what sort of *transformation* happens at the end, and what the character's psychological state was at the beginning, in the *pre-story* world. There are your three points of The Golden Triangle:

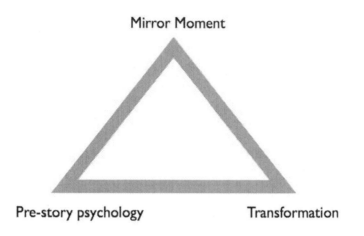

Mirror Moment

Pre-story psychology   **Transformation**

Pre-story psychology, and ultimate transformation, are the subjects of the next two chapters.

6. Before the Beginning

Knowing the all-important Mirror Moment, you can now go back before your novel begins and dig into the pre-story psychology of your Lead character. This won't be slogging round randomly. You'll be creating organic backstory related to that mid-point which is, remember, what your story is really about.

Let's take as an example the film *Lethal Weapon* (1987). You'll recall this is the story of two cops. One of them, Martin Riggs (Mel Gibson) is suffering deeply because his wife was murdered. He is so distraught he thinks about suicide every day. He just doesn't quite have the courage to pull the trigger.

This does, however, make him a super cop, because he doesn't care if he dies in the line of duty. So he will go into any situation with a crazy energy that freaks the bad guys out.

He is partnered with Roger Murtaugh (Danny Glover), who has a slightly different agenda. He wants to stay alive! Because he's going to retire soon and spend time with his wonderful family.

When they are partnered up, of course sparks fly.

There is a moment early in Act II when Riggs gets a potential suicide jumper off a roof by handcuffing himself to the guy then forcing a jump—onto the inflatable rescue cushion below.

Murtaugh is outraged and takes Riggs into an abandoned store to read him the riot act. He thinks Riggs is just bucking for a stress leave.

Riggs responds that not only is he serious about killing himself someday, he carries around a hollow-point bullet with him. He shows it to Murtaugh. He says someday he's going to use it to blow his head off.

Murtaugh thinks he's bluffing, and hands him his gun, challenging Riggs to do it right there.

"Don't tempt me, man!" Riggs says.

Murtaugh persists, and Riggs grabs the gun and puts it under his chin. Wild-eyed, he starts to pull on the trigger.

Just before the hammer falls, Murtaugh gets his thumb in it. The hammer clicks onto Murtaugh's thumb.

He realizes then Riggs isn't faking this thing at all.

Cut to the middle of the film. Murtaugh has invited Riggs over to dinner where Riggs begins to get to know the family. After dinner, as Riggs is getting in his truck to leave, he turns to Murtaugh and says, "You don't trust me, do you?"

Murtaugh laughs and says if Riggs can go another day without killing anyone, including either one of them, then he'll begin to trust him.

"Fair enough," Riggs says.

And then he tells Murtaugh something he's never told anyone. Maybe even himself, out loud. He talks about how, as a nineteen-year-old sniper in Laos (during the Vietnam war) he shot a guy from a thousand yards away in a high wind. Only a handful of guys in the world could have made that shot. "It's the only thing I was ever good at."

He gets in his truck and leaves.

It's the exact middle of the film. It is Riggs looking at himself in the mirror. Who is he? A killer. That's it. Nothing else. What will he become? He doesn't know at this point, and neither does Murtaugh.

But that's what the film is really all about.

Remember that hollow point bullet? I'm going to talk about it in the next chapter.

So if you were writing this as a novel, and you knew this was the Mirror Moment, you could spend some time building up the pre-story psychology of Martin Riggs.

You would ask some key questions and include the crucial fact that his wife was murdered before the story begins.

Where did he grow up?

What was his family life like?

What is his personality like?

What forces shaped his personality?

What was he like in school?

What was a major shaping event at the age of 16?

Describe in detail his Vietnam war experience.

When did he meet his wife? Describe the romance.

How was his wife murdered?

These are some of the questions you would want answered if you were writing *Lethal Weapon* as a novel. Now come up with similar questions for your Lead character. Give us her pre-story psychology. This is the bottom left point of The Golden Triangle.

7. The Transformation

Transformation is the final point on The Golden Triangle.

If you know the Mirror Moment, you know what your story is really about.

You can then formulate the pre-story background which makes the Mirror Moment *necessary*. Why? Because your Lead character will have to fundamentally change or grow stronger.

Of course, the Lead character can go from a positive to a negative pole, like Michael Corleone. Or refuse to change, like Hud Bannon (played by Paul Newman in the movie). In such cases, we have tragedy.

But if you know what kind of transformation you're writing toward, you can use that as a springboard to go back to pre-story psychology.

So you see that you can start at any point on The Golden Triangle and work your way to the other two. And once you do, nailing the Mirror Moment will guarantee your story has a solid throughline. Readers will feel it.

So what kind of story do you want to tell?

Write Your Novel From The Middle

Let's go back to *Lethal Weapon*. We know that Martin Riggs is suicidal, isolated, anti-social. He carries around a hollow-point bullet that he will use on himself someday. In the middle of the story he finally looks at himself and admits to his partner that the only thing he is good at is killing people.

You have figured out his pre-story psychology.

At the end, will Martin Riggs be transformed? That's what the Mirror Moment indicates. That's what this story is really all about.

After going through the death match in the story (physical and psychological death are at stake) Riggs saves Murtaugh's daughter and defeats the bad guys.

And he has found a reason to live again. He is no longer suicidal.

That's the transformation, but the key to this final point of The Golden Triangle is to *show us the transformation. It has to* be visual. It has to be a moment we could see if it were being shown on a screen.

That moment occurs when Riggs shows up at the Murtaugh home on Christmas Eve. The daughter he rescued answers. She invites him in, but Riggs demurs. Instead, he hands her a gift to give to her father. It's the hollow-point bullet with a ribbon around it. Riggs doesn't need it anymore.

Or that moment could come in an exchange of dialogue. The famous airport scene in *Casablanca* is an example. Rick explains to Ilsa why he can't go with her, why she must go with Lazlo, her husband. Why the problems of three small people "don't amount to a hill of beans in this crazy world."

36

And then, even further, when he puts his own life on the line so Ilsa and Lazlo can get out. Only a stunning reversal by Louis, the police captain, keeps Rick alive. He has been redeemed.

Creating Your Transformative Visual

Transformation is about change, and change needs to be proven. People can talk a good game. Someone can say he's sorry for stealing and wants to go straight. But until the thief returns the goods, we don't believe he's a changed person.

Change does involve an inner realization. But then, to prove itself, it must work outward in a visual form.

Scrooge, for example. He wakes up on Christmas Day. He begged for another chance. He told the final ghost he was not the man he used to be!

But has he changed? Dickens proceeds to give us the proof. Scrooge buys a prize turkey for the Cratchit family, sending it anonymously. He pledges a generous donation to the charity man he had tossed out of his office the day before. He reconciles with his nephew and his young wife. He raises Cratchit's salary and lets his clerk have all the coal he needs to keep warm. He becomes a second father to Tiny Tim. In fact, *He became as good a friend, as good a master, and as good a man, as the good old city knew, or any other good old city, town, or borough, in the good old world.*

Such a transformation needed to be seen, and Dickens essentially reverses everything Scrooge was in the first act by providing countervailing actions in the third.

Here is an approach for creating your transformative visual.

1. Write a paragraph of inner realization.

This should be a free-form, diary-like entry, none of which has to end up in your book, but of course some of it might. The main purpose of the exercise, however, is to dig as deeply into the thoughts of the character reflecting on the transformation.

Scrooge: I'm not who I was! They did it. The Spirits turned my heart of stone to a heart of flesh! I will honor Christmas in my heart, and try to keep it all the year. I will live in the Past, the Present, and the Future. The Spirits of all Three shall strive within me. I will not shut out the lessons that they teach! I am as light as a feather, I am as happy as an angel. I am as merry as a school-boy. I am as giddy as a drunken man. A merry Christmas to everybody! A happy New Year to all the world! Hallo here! Whoop! Hallo!

2. Brainstorm the actions the prove the transformation

Scrooge could:

- Sell all his possessions

- Buy a bracelet for his housekeeper

- Send a turkey to Bob Cratchit's home

- Adopt an orphan

- Become a second father to Tiny Tim

- Join a church choir

- Give generously to the charity he rejected earlier

And so on. In Scrooge's story, Dickens used several items. In the case of Martin Riggs, only one visual is given, often the best choice. If you can come up with one powerful action that sums it all up, so much the better. Thus, Riggs gives the ribbon-wrapped bullet as a gift for Murtaugh.

Note: You may come up with a great visual that seemingly comes out of the blue. But you like it. It resonates. So now all you have to do is *plant* something about that visual in the first act.

So, for example, in brainstorming Riggs's transformative act, perhaps the writer thought of that first. We can show that a suicidal cop is not suicidal by giving up the bullet he's keeping to shoot himself with. All we have to do now is plant a scene where Riggs shows that same bullet to Murtaugh, and explains what it's for.

That's the power of The Golden Triangle. You go from point to point, and then scene to scene.

8. Writing From the Middle

You now understand the three points of The Golden Triangle. The crucial point is at the top. The Mirror Moment. Once you know that, you can tackle the other two points: pre-story psychology and transformation. You are writing from the middle. Your novel has an organic unity. Your scenes will begin to fall into place.

Even if you don't know the scenes you're going to write until you get there, this middle core generates heat. The scenes you do write will be better for it. Even if you go off on a false trail, you'll start to feel cold. The Mirror Moment will call you back to the heat. And that's where you'll find your story again.

I can tell you from experience how tremendously freeing this is. Sure, there will be bumps along the way as you write. That's part of the process. But with your triangle in place, you'll know how to get over the bumps and blast through the walls.

No matter what kind of writer you fancy yourself to be.

Write Your Novel From The Middle

Are you a plotter? A pantser? A 'tweener?

You can use the Write From the Middle Method right now, or at any stage.

In fact, let me give you several ways you can use the method. Let's first have a look at the type of writer you might be.

Outliner

If you like to plot and plan first, the Write from the Middle Method will keep your structure solid and logical.

Go ahead and start outlining. My preferred approach is the index card method. I also use what I call "signpost scenes." These are scenes I know are going to be in my novel. There are fourteen of them. Here, in brief, is what they are:

1. • Opening Disturbance. Any kind of change, challenge, trouble, or difference in the Lead's ordinary world. The first scene.

2. • Care Package. Someone the Lead cares about as the story begins, part of the Lead's life in the ordinary world. Show the care happening early in the story.

3. • Argument Opposed to Transformation. A moment where the Lead states a belief that will be overturned at the end. This is the "thematic line." For example, Dorothy in *The Wizard of Oz* argues (to Toto) that there must be a place with no trouble. Far,

far away. At the end, she's learned, "There's no place like home."

(4) • Trouble brewing. Things may settle for a bit after the disturbance, but then a glimpse of greater trouble coming or hovering "in the air."

(5) • Doorway of No Return #1. Thrusts the Lead into the confrontations of Act II.

(6) • Kick in the Shins. In trying to solve the problem, achieve the objective, get moving, the Lead suffers a significant setback.

(7) • The Mirror Moment. (You know what this is. See chapter 5)

(8) • Pet the Dog. During the troubles of Act II, the Lead takes time out to help someone (or animal!) weaker than himself, even at the cost of more trouble. For example, Dr. Richard Kimble in *The Fugitive* saves the little boy in the emergency room, even though he gets found out by a nurse who calls security.

(9) • Doorway of No Return #2. Major setback, crisis, clue, or discovery. Makes final battle necessary and/or possible.

(10) • Mounting Forces. The opposition— knowing the battle is really on and that the Lead is committed—mounts larger forces.

11 • <u>Lights Out</u>. The darkest part of the plot for the Lead. It looks like all is lost.

12 • Q Factor. The emotional push that gives the Lead the courage to fight on or make the right choice, by recalling or seeing something of emotional impact from Act I, or hearing from a trusted character about the need to fight or choose rightly. (I call this the "Q Factor" in honor of that character from the James Bond films, who appears early in Act I to explain all the gadgets Bond gets to use. One of the gadgets usually gets Bond out of trouble near the end.)

13 • <u>Final Battle</u>. Outer (will Lead overcome the forces?) and/or Inner (will Lead make the right choice?)

14 • Transformation. Usually the last chapter of your book, confirming the character's change to stronger self or new self, and carrying the emotional resonance you want to leave with the audience.

Now, outlining friend, you can concentrate on the Mirror Moment, then proceed to transformation and pre-story. Or you can put your focus on the transformation scene for awhile, and then jump to pre-story and wind up at the mirror. It's up to you.

Just don't start writing until you have the triangle in place. You can always change it if you like. But I think you will be pleasantly surprised at how strong your novel will feel if you know your triangle.

Pantser

Go ahead and start writing. Play. Get to know your characters. Put them into scenes and see what happens. Write up to 10,000 words or so.

Now stop and ask yourself the key questions:

① • Who is your main character? What's her problem?

② • Does your main character have a moral flaw that is hurting others? If not, can you give her one?

③ • Once you have that flaw, figure out how she developed it. Go deep into her backstory to find out.

④ • Do you want to write a book with an upbeat ending? Then how will she overcome the flaw and be transformed? What will that scene look like?

⑤ • Do you want to write a downbeat ending? Show how your character has the chance to transform, but rejects it.

Come on, pantser, you can do at least that much thinking about your book! Now design a Mirror Moment for your character. A really hard look at herself.

What does she see in the mirror?

Go all out and write her inner thoughts. Write two or three or more pages of them. Let it all hang out. As a pantser, you know you're going to throw a lot of words away. So let these words flow, and then find the gold nuggets that express exactly what's going on.

Now you've got your Golden Triangle elements. Write to your heart's content all around the triangle. You won't be going haywire. You'll have a purpose. You'll have a throughline. You'll be flying, but toward a destination that has an appreciative crowd waiting for you. That crowd is your readers.

Tweener

Hey, borrow whatever you like! That's what makes you a tweener, right?

You can write the outline for your novel in two scenes: the Mirror Moment and the Transformation.

Add to that some pre-story.

You're good to go.

Or, you can use the Write From the Middle Method with an eye on the type of novel you're developing:

Genre

Let's say you know the genre you want to write. Maybe it's a thriller. What do you need?

You need a character and a situation. A concept. Come up with one. Put it in the form of a sentence:

My thriller is about a (character and vocation) who is (death stakes situation).

EXAMPLE: My thriller is about a lawyer who is stalked by the CIA.

Do you want your lawyer to be the kind of thriller hero who undergoes a fundamental transformation of character? Or do you want her to be forced into an extraordinary set of circumstances that forces her to grow stronger?

Maybe you're not sure.

Brainstorm possible Mirror Moments of both kinds.

Does it seem like she's got a moral flaw as she looks in the mirror?

Or does it seem like she's looking at the incredible odds against her?

Your writer's mind will give you one or two possibilities that click. Pick the best one. You can always change it later.

Now, if she's got a moral flaw, think about either the Transformation scene or the pre-story psychology. It doesn't matter what order. You'll get plenty of ideas as you think about it (and I like to think on paper for this part of the exercise).

At the end of all this, you'll have a solid Triangle and you're ready to begin writing or outlining.

Writing a romance? Well then, you have the lovers. If your main character is a woman, what's her flaw? What will she have to overcome to gain not only the love of the man, but grow as a person as well?

In the classic romance *It Happened One Night*, spoiled heiress Ellie Andrews has to transform from a selfish brat to a "real" person. That's the only way Peter Warne, her guide through the world of the common man, will respect and ultimately love her.

They find themselves in a cow pasture, next to a haystack. Peter is prepping some hay for her to sleep on. The screenwriter, Robert Riskin, has this in the script:

This brings silence, and he goes on building a bed for her. Then a close-up of Ellie shows her watching him. Her eyes soften. A very definite interest in him is slowly but surely blossoming, and the fact that he is making her bed adds to the intimacy of the scene.

This is her Mirror Moment, and it's done with just a camera shot. If you were writing this as a novel, you would fill this out with her interior thoughts.

It's easy now to go from this moment to pre-story (how she became a brat) and transformation. The transformation scene is when Ellie, in full bridal garb and about to get married to money, rejects that and runs away, literally, to find Peter again.

The key to using genre to write from the middle is to know your genre's conventions—the main story arcs involved—then formulate your triangle accordingly.

Character

Maybe you're a character first kind of writer. You like most of all to go deep inside a character and

47

show readers what makes him tick. Your stories tend to be about inner transformation.

There's your clue. Think about *transformation* first.

What if you want to explore how a character goes from being a nice person to an immoral one. Like Michael in *The Godfather.*

Think about the ending. Get a visual of the character *proving* the transformation.

In *The Godfather,* it's the final scene when Michael's wife, Kay, confronts him. She wants to know if it's true that he ordered the hit on his own brother-in-law. Michael tells Kay not to ask about his business, but she persists. So he allows her to ask this one time. He looks her right in the eye and lies. "No," he says.

Chilling.

What if you want to go the other way? You have a character who is isolated, bitter, amoral. You want him to go all the way to sacrificial at the end.

Like in *Casablanca.*

You brainstorm possible transformation scenes. One of them is a scene at an airport. You don't know why, but your imagination is giving you that picture. Then you see your character with a woman, a beautiful woman, and he's putting her on a plane. Why?

You brainstorm some more. Because by giving up the woman he loves most, even at the cost of his own life, he is saving something. What?

The war effort?

How?

Well, maybe the woman is married to a freedom fighter. Yes! She's married. And to a great hero! If your character doesn't give her up, he's going to be taking another man's wife and debilitating that husband, whose work will suffer.

Nice.

Now go back to pre-story. How did Rick (you've named him Rick for the time being) meet this woman? Where? Paris is for lovers, so that's a good place. What happened there? And so on.

Brainstorm these kinds of moments. It's fun. And you'll hit on scenes that excite you. Go from *transformation* to *pre-story* and then you'll be ready to go to the *Mirror Moment*.

Your novel will have a coherence that will serve you all the way through.

Theme

Some writers like to start with a theme, something they want to say about life, the universe, or everything. Maybe you want to say something like an existentialist philosopher: *That which does not kill us makes us stronger.*

Now who would make a good character for that?

Perhaps a woman.

Perhaps a young woman.

Perhaps a young woman who is put in a situation that spells almost certain death.

A woman like Katniss Everdeen.

What I would do here is brainstorm directly on the Mirror Moment. And it's one of those where the character realizes she's probably going to die.

Ask: what kind of scenario would that be?

Come up with some.

Come up with a lot. You get great ideas by coming up with as many as you can, and then choosing what you like best.

Among the scenes you brainstorm is Katniss right in the middle of a game that involves physical death.

A game? What kind of game would that be?

Brainstorm some more. And come up with something called the "Hunger Games" in a future, dystopian world.

So you design that Mirror Moment, then go to *transformation* and come up with a scene showing her newfound strength. Then go to *pre-story* and construct her world.

And once again The Golden Triangle works it's structural magic.

A Note About Parallel Plots

If you are writing a book with parallel plot lines, the Golden Triangle will elevate each one of them. If you look at the masters who do this—e.g., Stephen King, Dean Koontz—you'll see that each of their lead characters has this depth at the center of their particular lines.

The effect of this is breathtaking. Readers will be caught up in each level of the novel. The reading experience will be that much more compelling.

The rewards to as a writer will be equally thrilling. Have at it!

There it is. The basics of the Write From the Middle Method. The great strength of this process is that it is so flexible. It will never fail you.

Why not? Because no matter what you come up with it will *deepen* your novel. Whatever you find out about your main character using this method is going to make her a better character. Whatever scenes you come up with will be better scenes.

Readers will sense it. They will feel it. And because of that, they will be more likely to want to see more of what you write.

And that is how you build a quality career as a writer.

9. Some Writing Tips for Plotters, Pantsers and Everyone in Between

Let me finish this book with a few additional tips. Writing from the middle, and knowing the solid triangle of your story, give you a solid foundation that will serve you all your writing life. Now add to that productivity, great ideas, voice, and a never-ending program of self-improvement.

This is the way you build a career. I wish you well on the journey!

Tip #1 - Becoming An Idea Factory

It doesn't matter where your ideas come from. The Golden Triangle will guide you whenever you need it.

You get to choose. The power is in your hands.

But it all starts with an idea.

You have to have an idea that you can apply to The Golden Triangle. The great thing about being a writer is that you don't have to wait for one to come along and kick you in the butt. You can go out and get one, lots of them, and then use The Golden Triangle to help you decide which ones are the best.

Here's the process:

1. Get ideas.
2. Nurture the best ones.
3. Decide, with The Golden Triangle's help, which concepts to develop.
4. From your developed ideas, decide which book you want to write.
5. Write it.

Let's unpack this a little.

1. Get ideas

They're everywhere. Go get them.

Have a weekly creativity time. Half an hour a week at least. Go to your favorite coffee place with legal pad and pen (I like the freedom it gives) and just start thinking. To get you started, here are some of my favorite ways to go about it:

WHAT IF?
Train yourself to ask What if? about everything!

MEDIA SCAN
Quick scan of headlines, oddities, events. Use in conjunction with #1.

OCCUPATIONS
Research. Then ask, What's the worst thing that could happen to that person?

BORROW OLD PLOTS
A plot can be updated, or combined with another plot. Put new setting and characters in it.

COMPELLING CHARACTER
"Create a character with an obsession, then follow." –Ray Bradbury

PREDICT A TREND
Don't follow a trend. "I go to where the puck is going to be." – Wayne Gretzky

BURNING ISSUE
Key: Be fair to both sides. Justify each position.

TITLES
Create a title you could not resist picking up in a bookstore. Then just add the novel!

FIRST LINES
"You ever kill anything?" Roy asked. [from *The Voice of the Night* by Dean Koontz. All he knew was this first line, and the novel followed]

BOYS IN THE BASEMENT MORNING PAGES
Give your writer's mind some orders before you sleep. First thing in the morning, write down as many ideas as you can.

Keep a file, e or paper, of all your ideas. Throw nothing out.

2. Nurture the best ideas

Every now and then, go over your list of ideas. Highlight the ones you really like. These go on your "back burner."

From the highlighted list, choose ideas to move to the "front burner." I have a file called "Front Burner Concepts." These are the ideas I've spent some time nurturing.

Nurture means giving a little more focused attention. I like to use a page or two of freeform notes. I always type this because I want to keep all the notes readable and accessible. If I find myself getting really excited, I'll just keep writing and writing.

I call my nurtured ideas "concepts."

3. Decide, with The Golden Triangle's help, which concepts to develop

From my front burner file, I choose the concepts I want to develop. *Concept* is a word that comes from the land of movies. This is where scripts begin to get solid attention, talent is signed up, initial production tasks might be undertaken.

In fact, that's how I like to think of myself, as a mini–studio. I want to have a slate of possible productions. These go on my master projects chart. It's basically a corkboard—I use Scrivener software for this—on which I have my developing projects on index cards. I can move them around if I want to change the priority.

So just how do you develop a concept? Every writer should have his own approach. Here's a quick overview of mine.

One of the great writing books of all time is *Techniques of the Selling Writer* by Dwight V. Swain. On the development of concepts, Swain advocates the "white-hot document," basically writing as fast as you can with the idea gripping your brain. Write down possible characters, plot twists, scenes, themes, lines of dialogue. Anything.

Ask yourself questions. Why do I want to write this? What is it about my life at this moment in time that attracts me to this idea? Why would anybody want to read this book? How can I make this idea more interesting than any other handling of the same concept by another author?

Put this document aside.

Come back to it the next day. Read it over. Add to it. Highlight things that really stand out. Go down another track that you hadn't thought of the day before.

Put the document aside again.

Come back to it another day and do more of the same annotating, editing, and freshening.

Eventually, get this document into a shape that excites you and tells you this might actually be a really, really good book.

Now, boil it all down into an *elevator pitch*. This is where you want to be able to explain the entire book in the time it takes an elevator to go from the lobby to the tenth floor (and Spielberg happens to be in the elevator with you).

Write your pitch in three sentences:

First Sentence: Your Lead character's name, vocation and initial situation:

EXAMPLE: Will Connelly is an associate at prestigious San Francisco law firm, handling high-level merger negotiations between computer companies.

Second Sentence: "When" + the main plot problem

EXAMPLE: When Will celebrates by picking up a Russian woman at a club, he finds himself at the mercy of a ring of small-time Russian mobsters with designs on the top-secret NSA computer chip Will's client is developing.

Third Sentence: "Now" + the death stakes

EXAMPLE: Now, with the Russian mob, the SEC and the Department of Justice all after him, Will has to find a way to save his professional life and his own skin before the wrong people get the technology for mass destruction.

Elevator Pitch for *The Wizard of Oz*:

Dorothy Gale is a farm girl who dreams of getting out of Kansas to a land far, far away, where she and her dog will be safe from the likes of town busybody Miss Gulch.

When a twister hits the farm, Dorothy is transported to a land of strange creatures and at least one wicked witch who wants to kill her.

Now, with the help of three unlikely friends, Dorothy must find a way to destroy the wicked witch so the great wizard will send her back home.

Got it? Now you are ready to use The Golden Triangle to nail your story down. This is where you do it. This is the magic moment. This will enable you to write your novel from the middle outward, held together with a tent pole right in the center.

Come up with several ideas, expressed in one line.

A. Character Driven

Who is the character in the middle of the story? What must she become by the end? How does she see herself at this mid-point? How is this the critical moment in her life?

B. Plot Driven

How will the character realize he's probably going to die? What forces are against him? How will he realize it?

Play with both plot-driven and character-driven Triangle ideas. You may decide to switch from one to the other or combine them in some way.

It's up to you. The important thing is that you do it this way.

You are a development monster now. You're going to like the feeling.

4. From your developed concepts, decide which book you want to write

How do you decide what to write next?

It's up to you.

You can decide to write the concept that grips you the most. This is always a good fallback.

Or you can look at your top three or four and ask which one has the most commercial appeal. It's okay to do this. I have the quaint idea that writers are allowed to make money. Your decision won't be completely mercenary, though. If you've come this far with a concept you're already excited about it at some essential level.

Choose.

5. Write it

Remember Robert Heinlein's Two Rules for Writers:

1. You must write
2. You must finish what you write

You learn so much by finishing a novel. By fighting through the tough parts, by keeping on. You'll grow stronger as a writer every time.

The revision process for the finished novel is beyond the scope of this book, but I have already written the guide for you. It's called *Revision and Self-Editing for Publication* from Writer's Digest Books.

Tip #2 - Daily Writing on Steroids

I believe in the writer's subconscious mind. Stephen King calls it "the boys in the basement." There they are, down below, unseen and unheard but hard at work.

You have to treat them with respect, and also find ways to encourage their creativity.

I've come up with a system that I tried out during NaNoWriMo in 2013. It was inspired by something my agent and colleague, Donald Maass, did at the Story Masters conference where we (along with Christopher Vogler) teach each year. Before the students wrote anything, Don had them do some deep breathing and relaxation, wanting them just to be in the moment, feel what they felt, not force anything. Only after several minutes of this did he go into his famous prompts. Cool things started bubbling up.

Dorothea Brande, in *Becoming a Writer*, had a similar notion. For her it happened during sleep, and the first thing she would do upon waking is write, write, write without thinking, letting whatever was beneath the surface come to the top. That would be the material she'd work with.

Ray Bradbury did the same thing. He used to say he'd wake up and step on a land mine, words exploding, then he'd spend the rest of the day picking up the pieces—meaning, finding the story trying to get out.

So I started doing the following during NaNoWriMo, and it saw me through the completion of my novel in a fresh and pleasing way.

Write Your Novel From The Middle

1. Start with that breathing

I get comfortable, close my eyes, and breathe in and out, counting down from 20 to 0. I see the numbers as if on a lighted scoreboard. 20 - 19 - 18 and so on. If my thoughts start to wander to other things, I stop and start over from 20. The idea is to get to 0 with a quiet mind.

2. Keep your eyes closed and step into your story

Pretend you are magically able to walk into a movie screen and be in the movie of your novel. What do you see? What is your Lead character doing? Watch for a while. Let the images happen without controlling them.

3. Take notes with pen and paper

For me, there's something freer about using paper and pen to record what I've seen. Don't write in complete sentences. Make a "mind map" of connections. On the following page is a shot from my notebook, with notes I made on my WIP after doing this "movie in the mind" exercise. They won't make any sense to you, and you can't read my scrawl, but you'll get the idea.

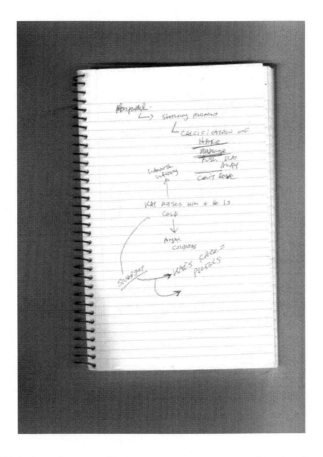

4. Think about the next scene you're going to write

Now you can be a little more directed. What scene are you working on? I have a structure for scenes I call the "3 Os"—Objective, Obstacles, Outcome.

What is your POV character's objective in the scene? If there isn't one, you're not ready to write. What obstacles will get in the way (conflict!)? What will be the outcome? (It should usually be a setback of some kind).

Then, as a recovering lawyer, I like to use SUES: Something Unexpected in Every Scene. Let your boys send up some suggestions from the basement. Write them down, even the strangest ones (these often turn out to be the best).

Do this until you get so excited about the scene you simply have to start writing.

5. Overtime

I want the boys working at night. So just before I nod off, I think about the story. I see the last scene I wrote. I ask, "What should happen next?"

In the morning, as fast as I can get to it, I jot some notes in my journal (this is an e-document I keep in Scrivener). I simply write down what I'm thinking, maybe ask myself a question or two. Then I'm ready to dive in for the day.

Tip #3 - The Key to Voice

You hear it every time there's a panel of agents and/or editors, when they are asked what they're looking for in a manuscript. Someone always says, "A fresh voice."

But no one knows how to define it. Over the years I've heard some attempts at explanation, and I've jotted them down. Here they are:

• A combination of character, setting, page-turning action.
• A distinctive style, like a Sergio Leone film.
• It's who you are.
• Personality on the page.
• It's something written from your deepest truth.
• Your expression as an artist.

Well, okay. I guess. But how do we develop voice? Indeed, is it something that *can* be developed? Or is it something you're born with?

What if you write in different genres? Is your voice in a noir thriller going to be the same as your voice in a romance?

Should writers even worry about voice? I counsel my students to be true to the story they're telling, true to the characters, and not to worry about this elusive thing everyone says they want. If the tale is well-told, that's the main thing.

But I do think there is something to be said for trying to coax out a little more voice, even though you can never quite nail it down to pure technique.

So what is it that does the coaxing? In a word, *joy*.

"In the great storytellers, there is a sort of self-enjoyment in the exercise of the sense of narrative; and this, by sheer contagion, communicates enjoyment to the reader. Perhaps it may be called (by analogy with the familiar phrase, "the joy of living") the joy of telling tales. The joy of telling tales which shines through *Treasure Island* is perhaps the main reason for the continued popularity of the story. The author is having such a good time in telling his tale that he gives us necessarily a good time in reading it." (Clayton Meeker Hamilton, *A Manual of the Art of Fiction* (1919)

I think Professor Hamilton nailed it. When an author is joyous in the telling, it pulses through the words. When you read a Ray Bradbury, for instance, you sense his joy. He was in love with words and his own imagination, and it showed.

I recall a *Writer's Digest* fiction column by Lawrence Block, back in the 80s, and he was telling about being at a book signing with some other authors, one of whom was a guy named Stephen King. And Stephen King's line was longer by far than for any of the other guys.

Which got Larry to thinking, what was it about King's stuff? And he decided that it was this joy aspect. When you read Stephen King, you feel like you're reading an author who loves writing, loves making up tales to creep us out, enjoys the very act of setting words down on paper.

Because when you're joyful in the writing, the writing is fresher and fuller. Fuller of what? Of you. And that translates to the page and becomes that thing called *Voice*.

So the question is, how can you get more joy into your writing?

Here are some thoughts:

1. Be excited about your story. If you're not jazzed about what you're writing, you can't be joyful about writing it. Dwight Swain, the great writing teacher, once said that the secret of excitement is to go deeper into your characters. Create more backstory, more secrets, more complexity, and you'll get excited again.

2. Write at your peak "freshness" time. Find out when you're most creative and awake and alive. Write for all you're worth during that time.

3. Take a break when it's drudgery, and do something else for awhile. I find that if I read a passage by one of my favorite writers, I soon enough get excited about writing and want to go back to my project.

4. Try a dose of Dr. Wicked (writeordie.com). This neat little program can be accessed online, or

downloaded to your desktop for ten bucks. Basically, it makes you write fast, because if you don't it will soon emit a terrible sound that will scratch your brain. Writing fast, without thinking too much, is fun, and many times you'll tickle out some of your best stuff that way.

5. Picture the reward. Now and then you need to daydream about your finished book and all the happy readers who are going to enjoy it—and who will put you on their favorite authors list.

You'll also find some helpful exercises on Voice and Style in my *Revision & Self-Editing for Publication* (Writer's Digest Books).

Tip #4 - On Showing and Telling

If there is any bit of advice that is ironclad for fiction writers, it is the axiom "Show, don't tell." Yet confusion about this aspect of the craft is one of the most common failings in beginning writers. If you want your fiction to take off in the reader's mind, you must grasp the difference between showing and telling.

That distinction is simply this. Showing is like watching a scene in a movie. All you have is what is on the screen before you. What the characters DO or SAY reveals who they are and what they're feeling.

Telling, on the other hand, merely explains what is going on in the scene, or inside the characters. It's like you are recounting the movie to a friend.

Another term used for telling is *narrative summary*. It's where you, the narrator/author, just tells us what happened.

Remember the scene in *Jurassic Park* the movie, where the newcomers catch their first glimpse of a dinosaur? With mouths open and eyes wide, they stand and look at this impossible creature before them. We see their expressions of awe before we, the audience, see what they are seeing.

Everything we need to know about their emotions is written on their faces. We are not given a voice in their heads. We know just by watching what they are feeling.

In a story, you would describe it in just that fashion: "Mark's eyes widened and his jaw dropped. He tried to take a breath, but breath did not come..."

The reader feels the emotions right along with the character.

That is so much better than telling it, like this, "Mark was stunned and frightened."

One of the best "show" novels ever written is the classic detective tale *The Maltese Falcon* by Dashiell Hammett. Hammett ushered in a whole new style, called "hard boiled," with this book. The mark of that style is that everything occurs just as if it were happening before us on a movie screen (which is one reason why this book translated so well into a movie).

In one scene the hero, Sam Spade, has to comfort the widow of his partner, Miles Archer, who was recently shot to death. She comes rushing into his office, and into his arms. Spade is put off by her crying because he knows it's mostly phony.

Now, Hammett could have written something like, "The woman threw herself, crying, into Spade's arms. He detested her crying. He detested her. He wanted to get out of there."

That's telling. But look at what the masterful Hammett does:

> *"Did you send for Miles's brother?" he asked.*
>
> *"Yes, he came over this morning." The words were blurred by her sobbing and his coat against her mouth.*
>
> *He grimaced again and bent his head for a surreptitious look at the watch on his wrist. His left arm was around her, the hand on her left shoulder. His cuff was pulled back far enough to leave the watch uncovered. It showed ten-ten.*

How much more effective this is! We SEE Spade glancing at his watch, which tells us just how unsympathetic he is to this display of emotion. It reaches us much more powerfully.

Too much telling is lazy

Here is an example of lazy telling from a bestselling writer. It comes in the second paragraph of the book:

> *She cared, she loved, she worked hard at whatever she did, she was there for the people who meant something to her, she was artistic in ways that always amazed her friends, she was unconsciously beautiful, and fun to be with.*

There are two major problems with this paragraph.

First, it is pure telling and therefore does not advance the character or story at all. Why not? Because we, as readers, are being asked to take the author's word for it, rather than having the author do the harder work of showing us the character in action.

Second, it's an exposition dump. There is no *marbling* of the essential information. It's just poured out all at once and therefore has no effect but dullness.

But you can't show everything

A novel that tried to *show* every single thing would end up 1000 pages, most of it boring. The rule is, the more intense the moment, the more showing you do.

Exposition Through Dialogue

Dialogue is often the easiest, most direct way to provide exposition. But it risks breaking the fictive dream if it requires the speaker to say something he'd have no way of knowing or he'd have no reason to verbalize (such as something everyone in the scene already knows). Thomas Sawyer calls that the "But you are my sister!" syndrome (in *Fiction Writing Demystified*). He advises:

Desperately avoid having your characters restate stuff they both already know, unless they're also adding something new.

When you use dialogue to convey expositional information, make sure it's believable—it sounds like something this character would say in this situation—and the character has a believable reason to say it.

Sawyer provides a couple of hints to achieve that: *oblique* and *indirect*. When direct exposition through dialogue is awkward (and it often is), look for a way to convey that information through implication. A mother and daughter would not likely stand around mentioning the father of the family is a policeman. But the mother might say, "Did you remember to pick up your father's uniform at the cleaners?" Or the daughter might say, "Mom, when everybody gets here tonight, could you *please* make sure Dad doesn't come rushing through the front door in his uniform and gun and everything?"

If, after all your efforts, it still feels wrong, look for another way to get that information across: in another scene or in the mouth of another character.

Or recast the scene so your character has a more believable reason to discuss that subject. Or consider slipping it into interior monologue.

Find three scenes in your novel where you give exposition in the narrative. Can you convert those sections into dialogue using *oblique* and *indirect* responses? Try it.

Exposition Through Interior Monologue

The opportunities and dangers of conveying exposition through interior monologue are similar to those of dialogue. Long passages of exposition, however presented, will likely feel tedious. And the same requirements hold: There must be a reason for the character to have these thoughts. Browne and King, authors of *Self-Editing for Fiction Writers*, say:

We once worked on a historical mystery set in a convent in sixteenth-century Spain. At one point, the main character simply sat in her room and pondered such everyday details of convent life as why the sisters were given the rooms they occupied. Technically it was interior monologue, but it was also out of character—people simply don't sit around and think about mundane details of life. In the author's next draft a new sister arrived at the convent and complained that her room was too small, and the information came out naturally through a scene.

There is generally a less-obtrusive way to convey exposition that's awkward delivered through dialogue or interior monologue. You can introduce a new character or give the viewpoint character a reason to think about those details, such as an unexpected visit from his prospective in-laws that causes him to notice the condition of his apartment. There's no point manipulating your plot or introducing characters just to insert exposition; make those changes only if they also benefit the story in other ways. Every scene...has to accomplish several things at once.

Find any section of your novel where your character is thinking exposition. Is it natural? If not, can you introduce a character or object that will introduce the thoughts more naturally?

Tip #5 - Secrets of a Page Turner

Some time ago, I had an exquisite experience, the kind we as readers love, but we as writers don't find often enough, namely: I got so caught up in a novel I lost the realization that I was reading at all. I was pulled into the fictive dream and did not want to put the book down. I set everything else aside so I could finish the book.

I can't remember the last time that happened. Usually when I read fiction part of my mind is analyzing it: *Why is the author doing that? Does this metaphor work? Why am I thinking of putting the book down? Ooh, that was a neat technique, I need to remember it . . .*

This time, though, I was fully into the story. It was only when I finished the book that I took a breath and asked myself, *What just happened? Why was I so caught up? What did this author do right?*

The novel is *Big Red's Daughter*. It's a 1953 Gold Medal paperback original. I found it when I was poking around the internet for 40s and 50s noir. I love that period because the plotting is often superb, the writing workmanlike to excellent, and the effect every bit as suspenseful as anything written today—without the need for gratuitous language or description of body parts.

And then I looked at the author's name. I didn't know him. So I did a little research and found out there's . . . very little research available on John McPartland. I love discovering little-known authors, and McPartland certainly qualifies. So how pleased was I when I got the book and had this "can't put it down" experience?

I'm not claiming that this is a novel that should have won the Pulitzer. But it is a prime example of what pulp and paperback writers of that era had to do to eat: write entertaining, fast moving, popular fiction. They knew the craft of storytelling. Since I teach it and take it apart myself, I was anxious to try to discover what McPartland brought to *Big Red's Daughter*. Here's what I found:

1. A decent guy just trying to find his place in the world

Jim Work is a Korea veteran, back home now and about to go to college on the G. I. Bill. The returning vet trying to find his place is a vintage post-war noir theme, one the reading audience couldn't get enough of. He wants a job. Wants to get along. Wants to find a girl and get married.

For a page-turner, you have to have a Lead character readers are not just going to care about, but root for. Even if you're writing about a negative Lead (e.g., Scrooge) the audience has got to find something possibly redeeming.

Jim Work is not perfect. Readers don't respond to characters who are too perfect. But we are on his side, because he yearns to do the right things.

2. The trouble starts on page one

Here's the first paragraph:

HE WAS DRIVING AN MG—a low English-built sports car— and he was a tire-squeaker, the way a wrong kind of guy is apt to be in a sports car. I heard the squeal of his tires as he gunned it, and then I saw him cutting in front of me like a red bug. My car piled into his and the bug turned over, spilling him and the girl with him out onto the street.

Turns out the other guy and girl are not hurt. The guy walks over to Jim and sucker punches him. He's about to stomp Jim's face into hamburger when the girl who was with him grabs him from behind.

The guy's name is Buddy Brown. The girl is Wild Kearney (her real name. Love it!) And immediately Jim is drawn to her—another noir trope. She is a "bronze-blonde" but "looked like the kind of girl that would be with winners, not losers, top winners in the top tournaments and never the second-flight or the almost-good-enough. Not the kind of girl that I'd ever known."

So here we have both violence and potential romance from the start. And the Lead is vulnerable both toughness and love.

The rule here is simple: Don't warm up your engines. Get the reader turning the page not because he's patient with you, but because he *needs to find out what is going to happen next!*

3. Unpredictability

Buddy Brown seems to calm down, and invites Jim out to a house where some other people are having a party. Suddenly, this Brown fellow seems like he might be okay. Jim goes along, because of Wild. And because he has a desire to work Brown over for the sucker punch, and maybe to start the process of getting the girl away from him.

Brown's behavior throughout the book is unpredictable, but with an undercurrent of danger. He's like a snake that could bite at any moment, but at other times seems friendly. You're just not sure what he's going to do next, because he is . . .

4. A nasty but charming bad guy

Buddy Brown is ruthless and sadistic, yet able to charm the ladies and the gents. At the house party Jim calls him a "punk," and Brown says he is going to kill Jim for that remark. Jim tries to fight him again and Brown beats him up, but good. We get the sense Buddy could kill Jim without a second thought, but then he relents and is charming again. In Hitchcock thrillers the most charming character is often the bad guy (e.g., Joseph Cotton in *Shadow of a Doubt* and Robert Walker in *Strangers on a Train*). Such a character is much more interesting than a one-note evil villain. Which leads to . . .

5. Sympathy for the bad guy

Dean Koontz is big on this. You put in just enough backstory to understand why a guy would turn out this way. The crosscurrents of emotion in a reader are experienced rather than analyzed, and that's a good thing. Great fiction is, above all, an emotional ride.

In one scene, Jim finds Buddy drunk and stumbling around, because he knows Big Red Kearney (Wild's tough-guy father) wants to hunt him down and kill or ruin him. Jim, in a display of 1950s loyalty to his species (sober men take care of drunken men), takes Buddy into a place for coffee. Buddy tells him a little of his backstory. When he was fifteen, growing up in New York, he and two friends got on the bad side of a local gang leader:

> He looked across the booth at me, his bruised, pale face a little twisted.
>
> "Mick and me, we run off from home. The boys came to my house and worked over my old man to tell where I was. He didn't know, so they gave him the big schlammin. He's never going to get over it. They caught Mick downtown somewhere and they took him out on Long Island, tied him up with wire, and burned him. You know, with gasoline. He was a very sharp kid, good dancer, lot of laughs when he was high on sticks. He got burned up."
>
> The slender, drunken boy was talking in his soft whisper, his eyes far away from mine, talking with a clear earnestness as if he were living it all again.
>
> "I've never forgotten that year. I hid down near the produce market, sleeping in the daytime, going

out at night to scrounge rotten fruit and stuff. The big rats would be out at night and I'd carry a stick and a sack of rocks. For two months I hid like that. Then it cleared up. The wheel got sent up for armed robbery and the other guys forgot about it. But I remember that year."

Suddenly Buddy is humanized. Not that he's any less dangerous. Our emotional involvement in the story thus deepens.

6. A spiral of trouble

In the first two chapters this guy Jim has a car accident, gets punched in the face, is drawn to another man's girl, goes to a party where he gets in another fight with Buddy, and ends up badly beaten and bloody.

And this is the good part of his next couple of days.

It's a classic example of things just getting worse and worse as they go along.

7. A love triangle

Between Wild, Buddy and Jim. And while we're on the subject, want to see how the best writers wrote about sex back then? Here is the only sex scene in the book, in its entirety:

I swung the car to the right on the rutted road over the dune, toward the surge of the waters of the bay.

It was a finding without a knowing. There had been a typhoon in Tokyo once when the wood-and-paper buildings ripped before the fury. This was a typhoon between two people—a man and a woman who thought she belonged to another man.

Then it was a knowing as enemies who were once friends might know each other.

After that it was a silence between two people who should not have been silent. We both knew now, we understood each other. We should not have been silent in that way. At last I held her in my arms again, and there was no storm, but there were no words.

We don't need body parts, do we?

8. A no-speedbump style

McPartland's style never gets in the way of the narrative. He doesn't strain for effect, and the resulting emotions are rendered naturally, sharply. After the sex scene described above, Jim takes Wild home.

She opened the door and was outside the car.

I was out and we stood there together. I brought her to me, but she was not with me. A tall girl in my arms, a lovely girl, a girl behind a frozen wall, a girl who did not speak.

Wild stood there after I put my arms down, and then there was a kiss, and we were close and warm there in the darkness, kissing as lovers do when the good-bye could be forever. Perhaps Wild thought it would be.

It was over, still without words, and she went down the steps and pushed open the door. There was a rectangle of soft light just before the door closed behind her.

I was halfway in the car when I heard the scream.

Do you want to read on? I know you do.

9. A relentless pace with a tightening noose

The action of the story is compressed into a couple of days, so it really moves. Any time you can put time pressure on your characters (the "ticking clock") it's a good thing. And the stakes, as I argue in my plotting books, have to be death (physical, professional or psychological). In *Big Red's Daughter*, it's physical. A noose (Jim is accused of murder) is tightening around the Lead's neck.

In the midst of the action there are emotional beats, too. But these never slow down the narrative, only deepen it. At one point Jim is put in a jail cell. Here is the longest emotional beat in the book:

THE NIGHT LONELINESS engulfed me. I thought of Buddy Brown.

They'd find him somewhere tonight. Walking on a dark street between the hills. In his bed. Sitting alone in his room with a bottle. Sitting alone and laughing, with the brown cigarette cupped in his hand, the weed-sweet smell thick in the room. Maybe now an officer, hand on his holstered gun, was walking toward Buddy Brown in the lonely Greyhound waiting room at Salinas while the heavy-eyed soldiers and huddled Mexicans watched. Maybe a state highway patrol car was flagging down the MG on 101. Night thoughts. Night thoughts on a bunk, scratching flea bites.

They wouldn't find him. It was a night truth, one of those things that you know as you lie awake toward dawn. Maybe they'd look for him, but they wouldn't find him.

I moved restlessly on the sagging bunk.

10. Honor

In *Revision & Self-Editing for Publication*, I have a section called "The Secret Ingredient: Honor." I think we are hard-wired to look for honor in others, and to want to act honorably ourselves when the chips are down. When Big Red Kearney shows up in the story, there is a bond of honor that he strikes with Jim, recognizing that Jim is not a punk like Buddy Brown. When this "male bonding" happens it makes you root for Jim all the more.

11. A resonant ending

I won't describe what it is, lest people want to read the book for themselves. The last chapter is short, doing its job. There is no anti-climax. And for my money, it ends just right, with what I call *resonance*. It's that feeling of satisfaction that the last note is perfect and extends in the air after you close the book.

I work on my endings more than any part of my stories. I want to leave the reader feeling like the whole trip has been worth it, right up to and including the very last line. I will sometimes re-write my last pages ten, twenty, even thirty times.

So there you have it. I'm not saying these eleven items are the only way to write a page-turner, but if you could get all of those in a book, that result would be practically guaranteed.

Author's Note

There's nothing I like better than helping fiction writers and screenwriters with the craft. I do hope you enjoyed this book and are as excited about writing from the middle as I am. Try out the method. Think about your novel or screenplay with The Golden Triangle in mind.

If it clicks for you, I'd appreciate your sharing that with me and others by way of a review on the store site of your choice (e.g., Amazon, Barnes & Noble).

Meanwhile, if you'd like to keep up with my writing books and fiction, you can sign up for my occasional update letter by going to my website, www.jamesscottbell.com.

And don't forget about my Knockout Novel program. This is a way I can be with you, helping you along, with any novel you write. It's an interactive program you can use over and over. All your notes can be downloaded for printing, too. And you can try it out risk free. www.hiveword.com/knockout.

Made in the USA
San Bernardino, CA
10 August 2016